The Radiant City

Sandra Florence

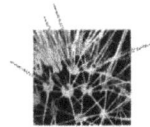

Jumping
Cholla
Press

Tucson Arizona

Library of Congress Control Number: 2015936849

ISBN: 978-1884106132

Jumping
Cholla
Press

Jumping Cholla Press
Tucson AZ

jumping_cholla@cox.net

Dedications

for my mother, father and brother

and to Brittney, Brian, Victoria and Lillyana

*

To my partner

Dianne Roberts for her love and support

*

And grateful acknowledgement to Philip Levine

My first poetry teacher who taught me to persevere

Also by Sandra Florence

Travelling in Small Steps

Chapbooks:

Recital

Almost Like Dancing

ACKNOWLEDGMENTS

I would like to thank the editors of the magazines and anthologies where many of these poems have previously appeared:

Sandscript, "Dress of Blue Leaves" and "Grief"
Thoughtsmith, "Nettles"
Gloom Cupboard, "Water Is the World's Consolation"
Amphibi, "The Baby and Her Shadow"
OVS (Organs of Vision and Speech), "The Radiant City"
Red Booth Review, "Grief"
The Blue Guitar, "There Was This Girl," "The Unbearable [White]ness of
        Being," "Dress of Blue Leaves," "Water Is the World's
        Consolation"
Travelling in Small Steps, "Epistle for Gloria," originally "No Ladder to
        Heaven"
Red Ochre Press, "Grief and Deception"
Ascent Aspirations, "Grief and Deception"
Penny Ante Feud, "Grief and Deception"

Special thanks to Donna Roberts for getting my work out there,

to Truda Stransky for her encouragement and belief I could complete this project,

and to Lynn Saul for her generosity and editorial wizardry.

CONTENTS

The Radiant City

Ars Poetica

I write because I cannot sing
and yes I can play the piano but the keys do not
respond to my touch as they once did,
witnesses to my streetcar song,
and one day I rode it all the way to the top of the hill
and passengers were pressed to the giant windshield
of the bus as it plunged down the hill on
Sacramento Street, and I waited,
a girl in a trolley suit
as the police cars circled the block
thinking they had spotted Patty Hearst,
but they were wrong,
generally speaking.
There was white space, white noise and anger,
little tear drops of it falling onto paper
like money which some said was a dog
of devotion, one I did not worship.

I write because my friends have fallen
in different directions in the grass
like empty cans or old lawn toys,
or balls of twine from a drawer
in my childhood home,
I want to keep it because of the smell,
and the texture which tightens and stretches
across space into a laugh.

I write because of the trouble I've seen,
lightning splitting the tree in half,
a little girl dragging gunny sacks too big for her,
through the cotton field,

her brother hanging in the woodshed,
an old lady curved into a rainbow of pain
praying to Jesus.

I write because of the clouds tugging at the ground
in the boy's poem   (he was from Chile and wore
worn-out boots and paint-stained pants, and his hair
was black with curls) and he loved Neruda
worshipped him, and now so do I,
maybe because of clouds or because of the braceros
in ten-gallon hats chewing the fat outside Bing's Diner
in the artichoke capital of the world,
or because of the shadows smashed on
the beach,
the sand was big,
rocklike pieces broke in my hands
cutting, wounding everything.

I write because sometimes the day stops
just as I enter the air
and even the tree looks vagrant,
and Anne's kitten of butter
sits on the window sill of the elevator
going up and going into the storm with
a bag of buttons, different sizes and colors
but something for everyone.

I write because
salt is a necessity, a currency, a life force
that cannot be stopped, can only be spilled
into an ecstasy between us.

Nettles

My mother wants to turn me into a stalk of wheat
and watch me grow in her field of vision,
a summer thing, the wisps of my hair flying,
my laughter sudden.
She wants to watch me spring like a swan from a lake.
Tucked into my white dress,
and all the other children in white.
She splashes us with camera light.
Faces I'll remember from photographs.
Laughter. The cakes and juice. The ice keeps us cool.
My boundaries are fixed like pins in a half-made dress.

***

My father starts the car and the field floats by
as he names the landscape: alfalfa, cotton, corn, sugar beets,
the landscape he has lived in all his life,
and now as we pass the fields,
he is strong, tall   brown,
he knows what the earth can grow
and what it can never give back.

***

I'm growing beside these two people,
a small stalk shooting up between them.
Sometimes their love falls on me.
Sometimes their love is a dark vein pulsing heavily
and I have no part in this except to watch
from my small distance that I can expand
by pushing against the car seat with my shoes,

scuffed and red. I listen to their voices.
My father twists behind the wheel.
My mother turns to smile at me,
to make sure I feel her happiness.
The flat land stretches for miles,
yielding its body to the machine,
and I try to understand their love.
To place myself within range of it.
Secrets hover between them
while I watch from the back seat
and out into the land sweeping past.
Silence....hours without words.
Sometimes he tells her she is beautiful
out by the sea in her dress like a wave.
I'm in my kerchief and jeans singing the number one.
The number is a bright flash of yellow sparks in my head.
I learn syllables and colors. A show of hands, a symmetry of three.

***

Through a half sleep of voices and telephone calls,
I feel the stillness. My father gone to work.
I see my mother on the phone. Her red lips moving
with words that might dazzle my ears if I could hear them.
If I could tell her how beautiful she is at this moment
having her secret conversation. I rise from my bed
tracing a path by the door and try to make myself invisible,
so I can come up on her words. I hide in a small space
only a child can make use of and watch her,
earrings, lipstick, scarf. Later, I'll decorate myself
with them pretending to be her. Later, she'll tell me about the birth,
the harangue and flash, my brother's white head emerging
from the dull pink insides of her body. I'll hear the crying.

This is some secret I was unprepared for
as I glowed in my little bed. As I slept next
to the plastic telephone ready to take messages.
A little soldier hoisting the dream flag.
The night has changed everything.
Suddenly, I'm a character in another story
while my mother and father hover
above their little pearl, not wanting to hurt me
with their new happiness, to blind me with their jewel.

***

A runny grey morning light wakes my brother from sleep.
His blue feathers sticking out.
He is a frightened-looking old man.
He is the man in the moon with a sagging mouth
and eyes that weep blue rivers.
It is January and I'm stuck inside with him.
He asks for my love, but I want to be out
in the trees and wind and wide-open spaces.
Bending over the crib, I wonder about his breath,
so slow and quiet. I put my fingers against his wet lips.
I sit in my dream shop and try to figure it out.
I watch the nurse ironing the diapers
and my mother feeding him. His milky face
relaxes long enough from crying
to drain my mother into him, and then he's returned
to his scratchy bed of ribbons where he sleeps for hours.
My mother blooms in her red sweater, gazes at me and smiles.
I go to his crib and look down at him. He's a pearl, a water baby
swimming under the roof of our lives.
My mother tells me how he came,
how he grew out of many women,

women who rode horses and wore starched caps,
women who read the bible and played the organ.
He entered our lives and changed everything
around him that was already planted and growing.
And the kiss that hushed me,
could never silence my brother.
He grips my fingers, and when he's older he'll call my name.

***

They take the picture and we win an honorable mention for the pose.
My brother staring up at me from his frilly container
and me bent over him, my fingers gripping the lace edges.
All the perfumed aunts sit with their gin and tonics
waiting for me to play the piano. The song is always the same,
the Moonlight Sonata. Every little girl should know it.

***

He hugs our mother's leg, pressing his face into her warm thigh.
She stands over the dishes. I hear a song rise from her,
As it drifts through the rooms like soap foam.
In the bathtub, little plastic toys bob against my brother's belly
and a moth flutters by his head, then drops its wings
into the white spokes of his hair.
I touch it, pull it from his hair and say, "eat this,"
and he turns his milky face to me and laughs,
trusting me, he reaches for it
but soon our secret is gone. The doors are thrown open,
things knocked down and the tub emptied of its contents.
All the little toys are sucked toward the drain
and the moth drowns in the swirling water.
We stand up dripping wet onto the rug.

I play the piano, my fingers exercising,
climbing the clock in the back of my brain
as it doles out its numbers. The wheels and pulleys
inside stacking up time. My brother waits for me
to finish my recital and pull him by the hand
out into the cold winter morning.

I wake.
The edge of night still lingers
as deep color pushes through. The color of my mother's robe
as she rises in the morning with her song.
Everything in the house moves toward her,
hands, my brother's hands like little paper cups,
his face asking. The perplexing color and tone of her brows.
I smell soap in the folds of her bathrobe
as I nestle there. I watch her untangle her wet hair.
Listen to the click of her slippers on linoleum.

The teacher plunks her cane along rows of children
Lined up for lunch.
My cheeks burn red as I wait to escape the cafeteria line.
My friends and I sneak out and make our way
through alleys to the back of a church where we hide.
We smoke bubble-gum cigars and eat candy bars for lunch.
Laugh,   thinking of the satellite above our heads
watching us with its huge eye. Has it spotted us
in our lavender skirts and white oxfords?
We explode with laughter.
Men in silver helmets bobbing weightlessly in the void.

The news. We hear it there and begin to see ourselves
at the long distance from our own bodies.

***

My brother lies on the floor sucking his thumb.
He doesn't want to start school tomorrow.
My father is behind the newspaper, a can of beer at his side.
I walk over and take a sip. I think to myself, *that takes guts,*
a word I've learned on TV. I say to him, "that makes my guts burn."
He looks out from behind the newspaper and says, "do you want a slap?"

***

My brother brings a pan of cold water into the front yard.
He takes each kitten and places it under the water,
holding it there for a long time.
Then he lifts it out, sets it down,
and takes another one and plunges it into the water.
The kittens mewl and squeal in their wet fur.
I watch for a while, then run to tell my mother.
She rushes toward him, grabs him by the arm
and tugs him into the house. Then she returns,
bringing soft towels. She wraps each kitten
up and pats it dry. The kittens are crying softly
now and so is my mother.

***

My mother and father have a fight.
She stays at home, fuming in her kitchen.
My brother slouches in the old armchair.
When my father and I leave, she won't say goodbye.

Now, I'm sitting in the cab of the truck, eating a Mars bar.
He stopped and got it for me. We're going to grandma's house.
My father is going to leave me there while he plays poker
with his friend Buttons. And they will talk about money.
Sometimes they talk about gold mines and oil wells.
We have one. My father drove us out to see it once.
We sat in the car in the heat, staring up at the huge rocking dinosaur,
swaying and bending its head to the ground.
We waited for the gusher, the thick oily blood to pour out.
My father got out of the car and squinted into the sun,
tilting his head back to stare up at the machinery.
He stared at it for a long time, then turned back to us, and got in the car.
He seemed disappointed as we drove home.
I wanted to say something to him, to let him know
I believed in the machinery, believed it could
make us rich like he said. But I didn't know how to say it.
And now, too. I keep trying to talk to him,
but I don't know enough about crops, farming and weather.
My words turn into hard little knots as I speak and he doesn't listen.
He just keeps driving. Man talk.
I wish I could be a little man my father would talk to.

***

There are eight adults sitting around
the table this summer evening.
There's a smell of tea and lemon in the rooms.
My brother and I run and hide,
getting ready for our masquerade.
We take turns fitting each other into costumes.
I place a black wig on his head.
He ties up the back of an old black gown.
I slip into my mother's old black shoes.

He pulls on a plastic nose
and some jewelry from a box she gave us.
We run into the dining room.
He sets his metal gorilla on the floor
in front of the adults. He shoots the gorilla
with his dart gun. It raises its arms, its eyes turn green
and it makes a roaring noise as yellow sparks fly out of its mouth.
We dance and squeal in front of them, trying to make them laugh.

***

My father digs twenty-foot holes
near the base of two trees in the front yard.
He removes the clay that is keeping them from growing.
He turns to me and my brother, and warns us,
"don't go near the holes."
When he's gone we move closer to the trees.
I stare down into the dark holes.
"What are you looking for?" my brother asks
as he swings from a tree limb. "China," I tell him.
He laughs and flings his body out over the hole.
I want the small path to a life I've never lived.
Roads and thoroughfares of people from strange lands
"The Boy Hero From Harlem"...
"The Girl Who Lived By Her Wits."...
"A Child in a Mexican Garden"...
The people I find in books, the books under my bed,
the books on the shelf. I grip the book to my stomach…
feel the warmth   smell the paper.
At twelve my heart is an encyclopedia.

***

My mother is on the floor doing sit ups.
Up and down, rolling back and forth like
a large ball of light. She's just come back from the
grocery store with a large bag of grapefruit.
A huge bowl of them glow on the dining table.
As she performs her ritual, she tells me she is on a diet,
that she will only eat grapefruit, until once again
she can fit into her wedding suit.
She's shown me the picture of her and my father
on their wedding day, both trim and fit in their gabardine suits.
But that was a long time ago. After she finishes her exercises,
she struggles to her feet and goes over to the bowl of fruit.
She takes one in her hand and walks to the kitchen.
She cuts into the juicy flesh, goes around each segment
with a knife, freeing the fruity insides.
A tangy smell hits the air.
"I love this grapefruit," she says to me as I watch.
She eats the segments quickly now, juice trickling down her chin.

***

In Los Angeles, we stay in a hotel near the
Sacred Heart Hospital and walk there each morning
to visit my father.
He's going to have open-heart surgery,
A valve in his heart is closing. The doctor tells my mother
he will stick his antiseptic fingers into the closing valve
and force it to open. This man will touch the pink flesh
of my father's heart.
I look at my father in his bed
with the metal sides pulled up.
He looks like a child in a crib, but he is thin and ghostlike.
He's lost fifty pounds. And quit smoking.

- 23 -

When he returns home weeks later,
he stands in the living room with his shirt off,
showing us the scar, a thin red ladder curving
around his shoulder blade. I want to touch it
but I'm afraid. Instead I dream of the scar for several nights.
It is wide, thick, blue, and the doctor is pressing his fingers into it.

***

My brother runs to school with his basketball.
He doesn't remember the roses on my dress
or the way I hugged him into the photograph
just in time so he wouldn't be left out.
The camera swung and struck its blow.
But my shape is changing.
My father tells me to get out of the way
so he can pitch to my brother.
My mother tells me to come down from the tree,
it isn't ladylike. She rolls me here and there
making me try on new clothes. The clothes are blind and invisible,
beyond any reality. I walk into the living room
to show my father, and he sticks his head out
from behind the newspaper and nods.
Then, he leaves in the foggy morning light for Chicago.
Later, he'll stand at the podium in his convention hat
and brilliant smile, talking about the farm land — how to save it.
Later, as my mother sits under her helmet at the beauty shop,
I'll pour myself a glass of wine and race back to my room,
back to the picture of that movie star sitting at a table
holding a cigarette in her hand. The caption reads…
"No, I don't believe in love.
It's just an excuse to inflict pain."
I breathe it in.

***

I return on Sunday to my grandmother's house.
The portable bible sits on the rickety table laughing at us.
I reach behind the couch and pull out magazines,
my grandmother's private stash…*Modern Romance*,
True Experience. I fall asleep on her chenille bedspread.
I fall into a trance, but not the one they expect.
But they know, my grandmother and her accomplice, my mother.
They have watched me for years trying to make sure
I turn out all right. They come after me armed
with their pamphlets on child rearing. They shake me and shake me
until I crack, and pop open….red and pulpy and new.
They tell me their stories, each her own side of it.
They want me to take an interest in the secret society of women.
And the geraniums. My grandmother points to them,
"see those," she says, "the soil is fit for nothing but geraniums."
They are resilient like her. Like I must become.
Their startled heads push up in the crushing summer light.

***

I pretend that the roses won't die.
I pretend that my grandmother won't die.
She goes sailing by in her wheelchair
toward the screened-in porch, whispering
some secret she'll never share with me.
I sit by her and read *Ship of Fools*.
She taps my knee, interrupting my reverie
and says, "don't ever get married." The house rocks
with her mysterious crippled movements.
I lift the medicine spoon in front of her
and she frowns at me. Shakes her head, refuses my offer.

"I don't need that; I'm too old."
It is the middle of July and getting hotter.
I step up my movements between the kitchen,
bedroom and sun porch. I roll her from room to room
so she can feel the soft breeze.
I sleep in the bedroom down the hall.
I close my eyes, and in a field not far from here, a friend dies,
the heavy machinery twisting and pushing his body into the earth.
My grandmother dies in her separate space,
quietly transforming herself into an enormous pink bulk.
Ninety-three years. We weep and bow our heads.
There's a story in the newspaper about her.
"The oldest of ten children"
"an early pioneer in California"
"crossed the frontier at two on an immigrant train
with her mother and baby sister, Sara."
Leaving the big red house with so many hiding places,
I take her Japanese tea set, her ring, and rosary beads.
The dark rooms collapse inward against time.

***

I step up and take the roses he offers.
The candy-apple Corvette shoots down the street
with me in it posing as a sweetheart. I wave at the crowd
and smile as the bands and drill teams
perform for the screaming fans. The parade moves along
the street in a flurry of confetti, balloons, and candy hurled from floats.
Later, as the street sweepers rake up the trash
our parade has left behind, I fall out of my party dress,
still pretending, and press my body against this boy's
like a glistening fish. We toss on the cold upholstery

as the fog envelops our car and lights flash in the field where we've
 parked.

***

We're dancing by the cotton gin. It whirls its cotton flowers at us.
We've escaped the tyranny of the high school prom and late-night dinner.
Instead we take a drive out along the curve of stars
that sweep the highway. Along a track of rails
reaching deep into the dark where no one can find us.
We swill beer, and run foot races.
The girls remove high-heels and dash down the canal bank.
The boys follow. This makes us want to run farther,
beyond ourselves, into the wide-open land of another time.
Four kids pile into the car as others watch. It begins to move
through space just above the ground like an asteroid.
Faster and faster the wheels flake away time and space,
rotating them into an iron animal, its wheels firmly rolling
in front of the car. It crashes into the side of the train.
It groans for a moment and drags the car along. Then, as if tiring,
The train shakes the car loose and the car slides into a ditch of dry grass.
One boy's face is shattered.
One girl runs into the road
waving her arms, ribbons of blood,
yelling words at cars that swerve to avoid her.

***

There are photos of me and my friend
on her surfboard in a swimming pool,
learning to balance. There are photos of my
boyfriends in their over-sized suits. Each year a new dance

and a new boy looking rumpled in his rented tux.
Until one year the same boy begins to reappear.
Blue eyes, blue tuxedo. There's a party that goes on for days.
Boys drag race on the road in front of the house.
Jimmy Hendrix on the stereo upstairs, "Purple Haze,"
a music I'm not used to, played over and over
until it becomes a chant, an incantation.
Beer bottles line the mantel and window ledges,
are scattered along the wall, a small pyramid of them
stacked on the dining table. Laughter from the dark stairs,
distant voices over the laughter and the screech of tires on the road.
For what seems like hours, I watch boys go in and out of a room.
I hear a girl's voice for a second,
someone hands me a beer
and I drink it down fast, gulping,
spilling some of it on my blouse.
The boy says something to me, and I lean into
his words and nod, pretending to understand.
But I don't. Another boy disappears into the room.
I'm drunk. My head is pounding. It's getting dark.
Most everyone has moved outside,
the music blasting into the summer sky,
then diffusing as the sky turns orange, then pink.
I go to the door of the room. My body is heavy as I lean
against the door. It opens. The girl who was in this room is gone.
I move around the room, a Letterman's jacket thrown on a chair,
a baseball trophy on the dresser, a surfboard leaning against the wall.
A few simple possessions to tell you about a life and how it might unfold.
I move to the window and see several boys in the driveway
challenging each other to race. My boyfriend is huddled over
the engine of a GTO. He and the others are raving about
the power of the machine. He is wearing a thin white t-shirt
and his arms are crossed over his chest, his hands

pressed into his armpits. His body shivers in the growing dark.

***

I want to go away with my headphones
and listen to "Strange Days." I want to be a freak,
one of those fat freaks. To shoot rainbow Koolaid
in my arm and glow orange. Instead, I must dissect this cat.
Marble-eyed, it stares up at me from its smelly tray.
I must find the long thread of bones,
pull them from its body and place them in a jar, wishing for its rebirth
and the births of so many being destroyed in this learning experience.
I feel sick now, an ache in my throat as I begin cutting.
"This environment," says the biology professor holding
the jar in front of us, "this organism includes God. The small god
that we laugh and blow bubbles at. It is beautiful.
The grasshopper, the clam, the fetal pig toddling happily
from side to side in its chemical sleep.
And this frog undergoing separation
from its heart that blooms like a valentine under glass.
And the sea shell inside me. Spiraling upward until
it presses against the base of my throat
creating a vacuum. This vacuum includes god.
The little god that will send me cards and letters
in the mail one day. The little god that will ask,
"do you miss me when I'm gone?" Twinkle twinkle.
The sky of my stomach opens. I am a nettle of questions.
I am a soup, becoming a stone soup,
with the little white head of god bobbing inside me.

***

The air is yellow and heavy as we drive

across the desert this afternoon.
His brother and sister-in-law in the front seat,
and my husband-to-be and I are in the back seat.
We keep our distance from one another.
He stares out the window at dust devils
and tumbleweeds, at nothing in particular.
I can't believe this is the same boy I thought I loved.
The boy I thought loved me. I can barely feel the
air conditioner, so I lean forward and prop my head
onto the back of the driver's seat. I feel like a little girl
with her parents, and if I really pretend,
can imagine that we are all on vacation.
We pull off the road at a dusty cafe. I go into the bathroom
and stare at my reflection in the mirror and want to cry.
I want to say, "this is crazy, I'm sorry, I made a mistake.
Let's turn around and go back." Somehow because his
brother and sister have paid for this trip
those words are impossible.
I leave the bathroom and try to eat.
To digest what is happening to me.
It feels dull and plain and my body aches,
and for the first time in my life, I think about my wrists
and want to make fine cuts along their delicate surface
and drain out this fear which seeps into me.

***

The minister coughs and the ceremony begins
and I walk twelve feet in my pink and green dress
to stand next to the boy who won't look at me.
He stares down at his feet ashamed, angry.
My wrists are aching now, and when it's over,
we quickly turn and march out of the chapel

- 30 -

and into the scorching heat. The afternoon is
still hot enough to lie in and tan, and I become
brown and glisten, think of the night ahead
and want a room by myself. A siren blasts out "I love you,"
carrying its victim to a safe resting place.
Somewhere between the swimming pool
and the cocktail hour, my new husband reaches
for me with his eyes closed and tries to forget
why we came here. Lying in Las Vegas on a white bedspread,
I hear the stars hiss and crack, a cluster of them
opening their hearts to the evening above billboards
and a performer gripping his microphone of tears
as bare-breasted women come out of the shadows
to dance for us.
And we go out into the night with a ring,
a push and shove, one body with its small accounts
of pain moving to meet another.

The Radiant City

(elegy for Dora & Lillie)

In the Radiant City there are books of poetry.
My grandmother whips the wind around her fingers,
moves through the grassy shade of Texas,
searching for her sorrow,
she has plenty   pockets full.

While I walked along the edge of this place
I hit upon something,
it was an old story about migrating across a landscape of dreams
things gone awry
my grandmother's beauty
lost in a cyclone,
flying trees and pieces of the house,
her being,   delicate and refined
burdened by wind and the Bible
she might bear this into another life
other lives   one after another.

But in the radiant city,
city of light and air
the intellect is a tiny dancer among leaves,
where is she now?   And my mother?

I think she runs through the radiant city a teenager taking flight,
a grown woman adjusting her hat and lipstick,
her jersey dress billows up into a cloudless day,
her mother turns the corner just ahead of her
between skyscrapers and a New York deli,
she hails a taxi and says follow that woman,

I hail another and say, follow her.

I'm running down a long flight of stairs through time in a radiant city,
I'm running along a precipice of grief, consoling myself
once my mother appeared in the bathtub in pink pajamas
once she appeared in the arts and crafts room and said I'm okay
once she appeared naked on the street and I comforted her.

Some old-timey tune is playing and we are completely out of place
in this terrain of steel and concrete.

My grandmother trudges up the stairs of an abandoned building,
waving hands grown heavy with scolding…
she looks furious as she climbs,
and yet there's a kind of serenity in her eyes
if you take the time to look,
she covers ground at a furious pace
a field   a meadow
a back porch where she hands out sandwiches to hobos,
bearded and luscious in their dirty jeans.

I reach through the radiant city alive
yellow pearl   pink sky slowly turning.

My mother was afraid of the city,
preferring the small town and country road,
flowers in beds to tulips in window boxes
a well- trimmed lawn to a crowded street,
but the Radiant City beckons us one after another,
the frightening plane lands,
the steel beam freezes   mid-air.

Laughter does not echo in the Radiant City,

it folds and falls to the pavement,
I see it fall, one movement down
to the paved street.

My mother's apron cracks open,
oranges roll out of her lap and settle in the air
just ahead of me now
she passes...

a lawn mower, rose bushes, a recipe book, scissors, sand, old shoes,
flyswatter, gardening gloves, a diary of her year-long struggle with appendicitis.

Her mother calls her from the stairs *Lillie, Lillie,*
the name falls to the floor below.

My grandmother is still working her way up the stairs
past the drafting rooms and map of the city,
where men and women schemed and planned
over morning coffee
beyond their intellects and their fear
into quiet intersections of light.

***

Across the street from my grandmother's house an old woman shakes out a
        dust mop.
I'm a little girl dreaming at the window in a neighborhood of old ladies,
each one having outlived her husband.
The flowers are chaste and happy
the paint is fresh   the street safe and hygienic without husbands

The widows peek out from their curtains at each other.
One widow sits on her porch rocking,

one waters the flowers,
my grandmother reads the Bible,
thinks of her children,
   she takes the switch and goes after them
   switching at their legs
   as they scatter into the trees…
When the widows turn back from the windows
each tells herself a story about the other.

A story can anchor us to the earth
quickly told
believed and shared,
while my grandmother is on the porch
a house disappears in a dust storm
a child drowns
a husband leaves or is broken by the field.

My grandmother brushes the dirt floor of the garage
tamps down the dirt, tamp, tamp,
her weariness and sorrow.

The widows gather their thoughts
they are sure of themselves,
as sure and steady as the earth,
the widows piece, fold, and patch
they heat, scald, and scour
they rake, hoe, and weed
they tamp down, press and iron
they raise the iron skillets into the air
clean laundry flaps in a dry wind
the white walls of the Radiant City
reflect back their work,
all that has been done

has been taken away.

A cupful of wind
a forkful of dust
holding us to this blissful toil.

To come from dust
to live in its embrace   to return to it.

My grandmother's words,
an alphabet of stone
her discourse a hymn, an angry prayer
that spins in her conscience as she
whirls on the ground.

She passes through a formal dining room in her starched, faded apron
the table is set with china and silver
a sheer   sharp   sterile beauty.

For a moment her husband appears in the doorway,
a young man in faded overalls offering her
an armful of oranges.
He disappears as quickly as he came
a leaf storm in the corridor,
My mother forms the word "papa"
but it is not enough to bring him back into focus.

Hymn, dust, logic
starch, water, glow
lights on a California highway.

A little girl dreaming at the window in a neighborhood of old ladies,
each having outlived her husband.

***

Beyond the high rises   space   a frontier,
light billows up   my grandmother reaches for it
catching it in her cotton bonnet,
it picks her up and carries her along,
a piece of paper across the landscape.

***

Camera   strike   blow   reel   swing   rock and
        groove
a jitterbugging dust devil sweeps the plains.
My mother aims the camera and it strikes a blow
the purity of light sweeps over an image
a perfect birth,
the image falls into the stunned air
like a child
and takes a breath.

In twilight I catch a glimpse of her,
I make a motion toward her,
she begins to turn toward me,
then continues up the street.

my father's hat floats by   tickets to a Giants game
a pair of flowered bell bottoms
red rover red rover   a sugar bowl   a tin of snuff

They coalesce at the corner
into a pile of glitter after a parade,
dazzling on the windy pavement in front of her,

she steps over the pile and moves on,
so small
I can hold her in the palm of my hand,
a miniature orchid.

She used to say I had surpassed her
she said don't dispute my words.

A teaspoon of lies,
a cupful of joy.

Her mother stands waiting for her
with a switch made from a tree limb,
tapping the switch in the dust.
As my mother approaches
the switch becomes a ribbon,
a ribbon my grandmother tosses out across space,
a signal
reaching for her
into this eternal moment.

Grief

Your mother in a pink dress will marry for the third time.
She searches for her mascara in the deep seat of a chair
and finds a little boy dripping egg on the upholstery.
Your brother slips on marbles, tiny planets on the floor.
In the dark
all you see is the red tip of the cigarette burning
and know at the other end
is your father.
And now your mother in the green lawn chair
waves through the dark
to a friend,
you and your brother
ride bikes
through heavy summer air.

You are standing at the edge of it.
Everything you have ever had and lost.
Why must we always lose our
warm cloth mothers,
our up-standing fathers,
must our sun-baked childhoods
turn dry and wear out?
Can't we keep our special
pocket knife
our glowing
front-tooth-missing smiles,
our bangs chopped off, uneven
scabs on both knees,
mosquito bites?
Why must even these graces
be swept away?

Dress of Blue Leaves

My boundaries are fixed like
pins in the border of a half-made dress,
a dress of blue leaves and summer afternoons.
My mother is at the sewing machine stitching the dress,
closing the apertures of cloth and color against space,
sealing the sleeves, running the white thread
across the borders of the dress.   The dress is whole and finished.
Now she is ironing the dress. A starched and ironed dress that falls
across my legs creating a shade in the heat of the afternoon,
the long silence of heat that fills the valley,
moisture diffusing sunlight and a door opening
somewhere down the street. There's a smell of clean cloth
and warmth rising from the ironing board.
Hemline, trim, border, edge.

My mother goes over the edges, the borders, again and again
to make sure she hasn't missed anything.
She is careful to press the edges down,
to know where one thing stops and another begins.
Sometimes she lifts the iron across the dress
and it touches both sides at once,
the part of the world that is only the dress
with its dotted-swiss trim, and blue leaves,
the long sash that will wrap around me once I am in it,
and the part of the world that is not the dress,
where the border dissolves away
where there is only remembrance and longing.

Yellow Cotton Shirt

A light breeze flits under the short sleeves
of the yellow shirt, and the sleeves billow out,
tickling his tan arms. His new young wife,
who is pregnant, awkwardly dishes potato salad
onto paper plates under the gaze of two daughters
from his first marriage. They watch from the edge
of the picnic grounds having placed themselves
as far away as possible. One lights a cigarette
and takes a long drag, then blows the smoke into blue air.
The other sits on a large rock, her knees pulled up
tight against her chest. He calls to the girls to come to the table,
to have some food, but they ignore him.
They smoke, hunch, turn away.
The potato salad is a pale yellow dollop
melting on blue paper plates.
His yellow sleeves flutter and fall, cloth birds,
yellow with blue wings.

Wayward

While my father tramps the levees,
my mother sings along with Gogie Grant,
a song about a man who is wayward, restless,
who travels in old box cars across deserts and plains, into mountains,
and even though I am a girl, I know the feeling, how it would be great
to get on the train and ride, watching the whole of civilization roll by.

I would swing up into the car as it slowed
with a little help from a rider and sit on a bale of hay
in the corner, be as still as possible not to call
attention to myself, in my overalls, long sleeved shirt and cap
like my grandfather used to wear. Some good work boots
like my father wears.

As the train slips past, I could wave to my dad,
a small figure walking the levee, but he is so intent
looking over the irrigation system to make sure the levees
will hold and the banks are strong, that the rain coming down,
an unusual amount for this time of year, won't leave the farmers stranded.
He won't look up or allow himself to be distracted from the caterpillars,
cotton pickers, and tractors he worked so hard to acquire.

He won't look up and he won't see me.
My mother will sing Gogie's song
in that aching throaty longing for some man
who is restless and wandering, not a real man, not my dad,
for my dad is not a wanderer, except in fields, on the levees,
a wanderer among the columns of numbers in the books in his office,
tiny rows to walk through with new growth promising everything.

Ostinato

There must have been a space between the weight of things
And the time the teacher insisted she sing the musical scale
rather than play it. The teacher was old and knew her discipline
and because of this had come from a city far away to live
on a quiet tree lined street in this small town.

The house was dark inside and kept the summer room cool
and made the intimacy of each lesson concrete; she learned
the dark polished wood, the rugs over the wood, the trees and backyard;
she did not see it, but repeated the stanza and realized her fingers
were not right, not fine enough. The stroll along the keyboard could be
learned, but first the repetition and her teacher, Mrs. Clark,
taught most of the girls her age who could afford lessons.

She had a feel for the andante and the adagio easing over
The dark places in the music and just when she thought she was done,
The teacher said, *again*, and she was off on the flow that seemed
As endless as the machine doling out its numbers, and she bent into it,
Not so much with her fingers as with her heart.

She became aware of the pressure that kept her seated,
The bench with its hard surface, and the old woman's hands,
bony and veined, waited to correct any violation. She could be still
and she could break into a bloom of notes at any moment;
she loved this weight which kept her in place, focused,
holding the notes and scale and the piano's earthiness
giving way to another world, elevated and lavish.

Etude

There was a shadow surrounding the house
although it was not dark,
palm fronds and large rubber plants,
rooms she didn't know and where she was not allowed.
Small figures of the great composers,
the white busts of Bach, Beethoven, Brahms
sitting on the top of the piano, lining the mantel,
were everywhere watching her, and there was nothing
she could do about it.

Her fingers ached from playing the same keys while the teacher
stared into the afternoon, a bass clef of earth and granite bones,
footnotes in her throat. There were spring waves before the heat
and the girl twisted inside the music, a treble of laughter. She was ready
to go by herself note by note, pulling half by half. A car going by
spoiled the piano teacher's reverie. The old woman's fingers
still limber but becoming wax heavy. The Etude, like the breath,
was complex, perhaps beyond the girl's technical skill; she held
her breath under a falling octave, but the teacher insisted
she keep going and now she stretched herself, found herself
in a landscape of black and white, an ecstatic cluster of light,
she and the teacher in a strange fusion, becoming atonal dust.

Kay Jones

After three years in the old Victorian off Main Street,
it was onto a new music teacher, in a ranch style home
with sliding glass doors, who sometimes let her students
play popular music. Before her son David came home
in his plaid cowboy shirt and ran down the hall to his room.
The girl played until it was dark outside and she would
call her mother to say she was walking the two blocks home.
She had managed the Ecossaise but would not play it for the recital
because she was, according to Kay Jones, better at emotional
interpretation than her peers.

Kay Jones was beautiful with long brown wavy hair,
blue eyes and hands that were perfect and white. They flooded the keys
with a frenetic joy, even the trivial popular pieces like the Starlight Waltz
became vital under her touch. And so the light-hearted, fast-paced
pieces would go to someone else, while she struggled with weight,
doubt and complexity.

My Father Is Singing

My father is singing in an oak tree behind the house.
His sisters are somewhere in town taking voice lessons;
their voices crackle and fall into the corners of the room.
The teacher taps her baton against the music stand as
though to redirect the odd sounds, the off-key notes.
The girls want to flee the scene of their musical crimes;
they know they can't sing, neither together or apart.
They are girls and they must have lessons.
He's a boy; he cannot. Soon they'll run down
the cracked summer sidewalk and just as they enter
the house, his voice floats like a wave of cream into the leaves,
light and full of melody it rises without effort into the sky,
then gets trapped in the branches of the oak.
His voice is becoming solid and deepens with the
heaviness of summer. He is thin, wiry; no one would think
a voice like that could come out of such a fragile boy,
a boy with scars on his heart. When the girls return they
climb into the branches of the oak tree, each takes a limb.
My father takes one of the lower limbs, but a bigger
sturdier one and stands with both hands on his hips,
for balance and to help his breathing.

Like This

It's like when your father held you in his arms at the train station.
You were two and he'd taken you to say goodbye to Leonard Illisinga,
a man with a musical name from a country called Ceylon.
He'd come to the U.S. to study agriculture and he and your father became
        good friends,
worked long hours,
        walked the fields,
                drove the levee.
The machines hummed all morning in the mist of irrigation.
Great green fields glistening wet.
The small town weighted by water and heavy air.
Farm workers moved gracefully through the fields,
their old cars lined the roads
        filled with sleeping children.

Your father walks the cotton fields. Leonard walks with him.
Bends down to examine the bulbs. Tufts of bloom on rough stems.
It's always like this when you think of them together,
One from America,
      a big wide-open country.
One from a small island country,
        jungle, heat,
           iguanas curling in sunset trees.

Your father and Leonard pass farm workers as they chop at weeds,
dig into the earth,
        stake out a territory for cotton.

Leonard steps onto the train platform.
In the photograph he is holding you in his arms,
a dark man in a gray suit and white shirt,

he is smiling at you.
Your father buys the ticket to Los Angeles
where Leonard will go to a convention.

You, your father and Leonard in the truck driving the levee across land.
Westlake, Boswell, Crockett and Gambogi,
corporate land,
        windmills and water towers,
                        dry river beds and fields of cotton
where one day at a high school reunion a friend will tell you
they have the technology to grow colored cotton,
        blue   pink   brown.

But for now it is simple.
Your father telling Leonard about
John Deere and International Harvester,
Irrigation,
        pesticides,
                        crop dusting.

The duster swoops over the truck as it totters
on the levee, kicking up dust,
your father waves to the pilot
as he narrowly misses the telephone wires,
trying to give you a scare.

But nothing can scare you now.
Only the loss of someone you love
which has not yet happened.
Now you are collecting,
        gathering your treasures,
                        your people.
Their bright faces surround you,

mirror back what is real and important.

It is always like this when you think back or look at the photographs.

Leonard will stay for one year.
When he returns to Ceylon
he will write letters for the next twenty-five years
in a handwriting so small your father will use a magnifying glass to read
        them.

For now
when he comes to your house for dinner
he sits in your father's big chair,
your father takes the sofa.
Standing in front of him
in your white dress and sandals,
you are two,
the brush in your hands is big
with large plastic bristles.
Your father bends his head down so you can reach him
And you reach up and begin brushing his hair.

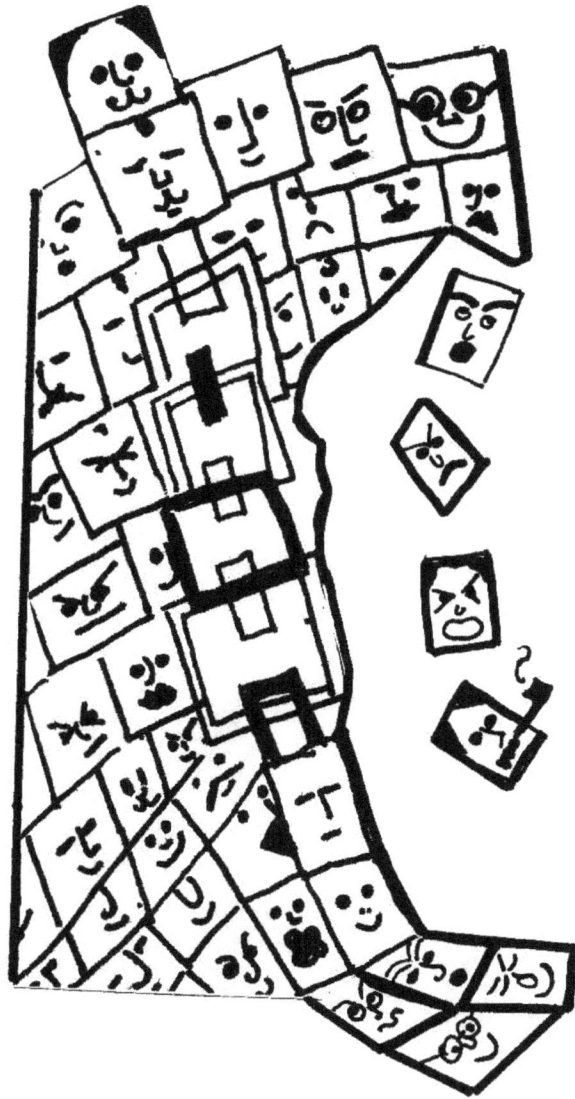

Neighbors and Fences

How we were then,
houses packed tightly after the war,
separated only by a waist-high fence
where my brother and I balanced,
pretending to be spies,
watched her hang laundry behind the garage
in careless shadows above the grass,
a cigarette pressed tightly between her lips.

How we are now,
I'd call her, but a Christmas card came back
marked "expired" and now her ex-husband,
    (who she left for a man with five children
    because she had been paralyzed and could not have her own)
has a whole new life after grieving her departure for twenty years.

After she left him,
he sat at Chicks Club every night
cursing women, getting drunk,
then drove home
to fall out of his car onto the front lawn
where he slept till morning,
when a neighbor might find him
and help him inside,
his house empty except for Pal, his only friend,
a little black dog he took on fishing trips to the coast
    (but gave away as soon as he met and married
        a wealthy woman with expensive furniture,
           and no room for a dog)

Slats of light cut across the lawn,

my brother hops the fence to get the ball,
finds the grieving husband on the lawn
        his clothes soaked with dew,

And unable to believe this was the man who had promised
to take us flying, the photographer
who took pictures of crop dusters, pilots,
and the war,   we would run to get our mother or father.

And while the husband grieved,
she was in another state, at a diner,
making the breakfast crowd laugh.
        She could, you know.
Everyone loved her.

My brother and I balanced on the fence
in front of her windows.
Pretending.
The fence was our world of danger.
The yard, a cool plane of green light
where we were extraordinary.

There Was This Girl

There was this girl whose history was fairly
golden in that she had everything she ever
wanted up until the time she didn't.
What transpired was the girl borrowed
her dad's car one foggy afternoon,
put 50 cents worth of gas in it,
enough to drive up and down Main St.
and then she took a detour.

At the same time her mother and father were
getting out of the car in another town to
see the sights, to buy a lamp, to do something
together that would bring them closer to each other.

There was this girl who sat on the porch as it
rained and the sky poured puddles of color
into the streets, and a brother who threw
the basketball against the garage door and
each time the girl was still and quiet,
a car sped by, a horn honked, the basketball slammed
against the wood, her parents appeared
as if they'd never been gone.

There was this girl across town
in another house, neglected,
a nurse mother always working,
three younger sisters,
and a police chief father who cared little
about the life of girls.

There was this place. A small square of light,

high grass, an abandoned car and this girl
would go to wait for her friend and smoke cigarettes
at the same time across town
her friend was shoved by the father,
held in place by the sisters.

As one girl smoked,
the other waited for gravity to release her,
and the girl would wait while rain made
pinging noises on the roof
and her friend would come with excuses, always late
and this girl would take note, light a cigarette for her friend,
touch the mark, barely visible.

At the same time the earth wished them well.
It wished them stillness, joy, soft smoky wind,
a place on the landscape to return to at the same
time there were other versions of the story.

We can know things without
asking, without knowing. How did this girl
know some part of her friend would be
lost, be irretrievable. There would always
be excuses at the same time there were
explanations piling up or interpretations
or critical breaches of trust. The split in
this girl, in her thinking one thing and
doing another, for example, allowing
herself to be violated while still believing in love
making mistakes, asking questions no one would answer.
About loss. About love.

There was this girl who had everything she

wanted at the same time things slipped
away. There was this girl and at the same
time a brother who played basketball and
excelled in math. There was this girl in her
sunny dress and her friend across town in
another house.
Two homes, mothers, fathers, sisters,
and a brother, and these things were
gathering into what they were
and at the same time what they would be.
As this girl sees them and her friend sees them.

The Unbearable [White]ness of Being

with gratitude to Milan Kundera

My whiteness is the rake and hoe
the blistered hands of a fifteen-year old girl,
chopping cotton to earn summer spending money,
it is the harsh voice and scowl
of the work crew foreman,
her need to exercise the little power she has.
In the field at dawn,
I look down the long row into an eternity of cotton.
Blue sky will soon burst open.

Three Mexican women with short hoes
chop weeds in the row next to me   never looking up,
to look up is to lose time   rhythm
each slice so precisely aimed
only a small puff of dust rises
they move quickly along the row
and soon I am looking at their bent backs.
They speak in Spanish
the continual hack hack of the hoe,
their synchronized movement forward,
their language,
all create a border
I will not be able to cross.

My whiteness exposed to burning blue…
their brownness enveloped by earth.
Drink   drink…   the water isn't enough to take away
my thirst, my isolation.

At ten o'clock we leave the field.
The three women get into an old car
and the rest follow in the foreman's van.
The road unfolds like a bolt of cloth
all the way to the sky...a blue blindness.

Up ahead the old car turns
into a row of Quonset huts near the canal.
As we pass them, I pretend not to see the camp and its people,
but I have always known they were there —
at the edge of town, the edge of vision.
> *An old woman sits in a broken window,*
> *the canal a trapped and foreign river.*

At home, my mother examines my hands,
the skin so sore I can barely move them.
She rubs salve into my palms
spreads it over my fingers
tells me I've done enough, earned enough.
And in a few days
my hands will have healed,
but the dryness has cut deep.

I return to my real life
white girl reading the signs
of transiency and migration
in a small farm town in the San Joaquin Valley.
I steal a look from time to time
at the other part of the world,
and when I turn back,
I drift.

Tomorrow Land

No time like the present to look out over
the wide vista of tomorrow in Tomorrow Land
where the snazziest thing used to be a space man and rocket ship,
and the stories our teacher read were not in color but were
the muted tones of metal undergoing transformation.

Tucked among the trees, a ruined paradise of recycled toys,
utensils, and comic books, a girl sits drawing pictures of her future.
With the picnickers packing up their baskets of fruit and potato salad,
and calling to us kids who blink like tiny lights in the trees
and we come down from the trees and run into our parents' arms,
but not before one more time around the lake chasing
the squawking geese trying to nibble up our discarded hot dogs.

In some dreams the water runs over everything,
it seeps up over the rocks and channels and
onto the steps and begins to filter under the doors like light.
This light is everything you have ever dreamed of,
the pink clouds in a gray landscape,
the soft rain coming down in the sun
so the rain looked gold.

Why are we still afraid when everything tastes so good,
like boysenberry pie,
doesn't make sense when our mother's dress
smells like a wave in the dark night.
And the dress becomes high and wide,
begins to curl and tilt and my brother and I are caught
in the tilt of her, the aim of her eyes
and the incline of her smile, and we begin to slide
into the curling wave, dizzy with its speed hurdling to the shore.

Idyll

My father and I sit next to each other at a large table in a café.
We have come on a bus to the valley to find a school.
We are the same age, very young, perhaps twenty.
He tells me that college was the time he felt the most free.
There is green everywhere, the fields are emerald,
even the food, mostly desserts, piled high on a lazy Susan,
is green and frosty. There are books stacked in an alcove
of the restaurant where we have stopped, and my father is reading
Kipling or the *Idylls of the King*.
I imagine him in an old Kipling storybook,
his dark wavy hair and dark skin glistening in the sun, a thin young man
running through wet leaves. I notice how smooth his face is.
How he holds the book up close and is so engrossed in the story.
He offers to tell me the story of what he is reading.
Then I remember the book,
with its faded yellow cover, all the books in the alcove are cloth,
and have a sweet old papery smell, and as he reads the sweet old papery
smell falls out of the book in so much golden dust.

Sphere

"It's a tiny sphere," my father said. He was a tall man with a deep voice.
"If you sleep with it next to your heart, you won't be afraid."
What did he mean, sphere? We studied circles and squares in school.
His explanations were so different. What was this magic sphere trick?
Parents always play tricks on their children, telling them about magic.

Gulp! I gulped the last of my coke, headed for the bedroom
where my fancy hi-fi system waited. Now that's magic;
it can do neat things lots, lots, lots, so much I can't keep track.
Pin-ball, drink dispenser, night-time lullaby playing all the latest tunes.
Wish I was grown up and could get all the slurpies I want.

Sometimes I can't find my socks. Neither can my dad.
He tries but things don't always match. But he says, "I got two. I got two.
So where's the other purple one?"

Two Kinds of Cold

She walked backwards over the sand
it was hot and burned the bottoms of her feet.
She was entranced but then there was pain
and she had to run to the water's edge to cool the burn.

It was always numbingly cold when they swam in the sea.
She and her brother stood at the edge,
shivered as goose-bumps covered their bodies,
and then they slipped under until they were completely
wet and the numbness set in. There was that small span
of time in which they could swim and raft without feeling a thing.

She was a child walking backward over sand,
cool one minute and hot the next until it stuck
to the bottoms of her feet like brown sugar.
She walked creating ruts that filled instantly with the sea
so they were gone soon and no one
could find her as she disappeared into the dunes.
Later, something tipped over and started melting.

There was something hard and cold at the edge and she was three.
She skittered across the sand into the sky but that was in her dream.

Now   in her waking life, a trip over the Sierra Nevadas
across slick mountain roads and trees that dripped resin
onto ancient ground; they stopped at the historic marker,
and got out to pay respects to the Donner Party.
The wind came up throwing the sharp smell
of pine and eucalyptus in their direction,
and so they went back to the car.
Her feet were numb inside her shoes.

She and her brother in the backseat
tried to wriggle their cold toes to life.
In the front, their mother tried to get the heater going.
Their father picked up speed,
passing cars on dangerous mountain curves.

The Professor of French History

With
a perfected nonchalance
the professor tiptoes barefoot
across the pool deck
and later
appears in the classroom,
hair still damp from his swim.

He pauses...
passes a casual glance
up and down
the classroom...
his students,
from various coastal cities
in California
believe the answers will
miraculously appear
at the time of the exam.

He reaches for his history book,
remembers
marrying the girl from France
in a hasty ceremony...
her mother calling from
the thorny rosebushes
just as the music began...
not to disturb his yearning heart
but to instruct,
the old woman
in an artful moment
took him aside

reminded him of their history,
their dreams tied
to the economic disadvantage of others
little shops in Montmarte,
soldiers returning from countries without names
where shoe laces were luxuries,
the ground of obligation intruding,
and so he took out the mortgage,
bought the car,
assembled the family
for a portrait.
These things will not be on the exam
yet,
he remembers the hill
in war torn France,
flags raised,
hearts lifted,
a surge of defiance
against a wind of tyranny,
this classroom,
this marriage
and the smile of a French woman.

Three Infatuations

First there was this Scandinavian beauty,
my camp counselor
with deep blue eyes
and blonde hair, a slight lisp that made her
more appealing,
we strolled along the lake and took
photos of each other in our baggy plaid
bermudas, after campfire
she leaned over to say goodnight;
her thighs winked at me from above.

My boyfriend came up on visitor's Sunday,
and we sat in the car eating fried chicken as it rained.
She pressed up against the car window
in her wet t-shirt,
mimicking a kiss,
we laughed, she pulled away,
but her lips stayed, imprinted on the window,
then she was gone,
her sneakers squishing on wet pine needles
as she walked away from the car
        (eventually to South Africa where I can
                only imagine she lived on a coffee plantation
                        and inadvertently supported apartheid)

                        ***

and then,
The Singing Nun came on and I reached for him,
his hard mouth and hands,
his scratchy crew cut against my cheek

a boy who would drink himself to death,
he wrote letters from the beach saying
he was "stoked on me."

The ocean a slice of cold blue
crashing white,
where he rode his board on jagged waves,
bragged about all the girls he got,
and I was long-haired and landlocked
and he and I would
go to the Mardi Gras together
with two other couples packed tightly
into someone's daddy's car
and before the dance
drink beer,
make out,
the boys trying desperately
to feel us up through our
thick satin dresses.

Afterward,
there would be a steak dinner
at the Imperial Dynasty,
one of the best restaurants in the valley,
certainly the best egg foo yung…
owned by a Chinese family of mysterious
and quixotic circumstances,
smugglers, back street scholars
priests…their pagoda hidden
on an alley where they practiced their arcane rituals
behind bamboo screens,
while just on the other side
drunk teenagers dragged main street

blasting *"I can't get no satisfaction."*

Then there was another girl,
completely the opposite of all this kid stuff.
In her tight black skirt
she danced dirty with her boyfriend,
gyrating a slow slinky sex,
and then her sudden disappearance from school
whispering in the halls
and the boy gone off to the army,
silent   invisible.

Much later,
after her marriage to a handsome grocery checker
with pale eyes and an overly-sweet smile,
a man most women found attractive,
in her kitchen getting drunk
while the scalloped potatoes burned
the boys outside barbecuing,
she told me what I already knew
she was unhappy years after the loss,
and her unhappiness bothered me,
the boredom of the perfect little house
and tidy kitchen,
a play house with nothing to take care of,
and I wondered
about the baby's father now
a poor boy,
not handsome, with a sad gentle face,
no one wanted her to marry,
but whom she said she still loved.

Flowers

A gorgeous tight-lipped boy in pencil thin pants,
fingers going up the legs of a girl even when
he didn't want to, not really.
And neither did she want to, but her dress was
fluttering under the tree, her feet in wet grass
and there were only a few such boys she'd
ever want. And only for short periods of time,
when the evening was a perfect blue and summer
wind blew across the boy's bare chest tickling
them into the nameless night, a necklace of lights
on the unfettered lawn, drops of pure rose nakedness.

Young

(for T)

There's nothing like going around in a wet bathing suit
all day with suntan lotion on your skin,
you smell like Coppertone and Chap Stick,
your hair is wild and stiff from water and wind,
your skin is bronzed and you spend so much time
lying in the sand at the beach one week with your
girlfriend Taffy, trying to act cool so Steve Oliver
will take you out on his board to show you how to surf
and you catch a small wave and ride it to shore and that's it,
you're back on the beach, Steve is showing another girl
how to surf and you feel your legs burning
and Taffy's older sister says to cover up
and stop complaining so you do.

At dinner, she asks you to chop mushrooms for a salad,
you're embarrassed because you've never eaten
one, so you stall in the bathroom long enough
to avoid the task but not the embarrassment
because Taffy's sister calls you *lame,*
then you and Taffy will borrow her father's car
and go to Sharon Todd's house
because she's freaking out over her boyfriend
Nummy who is possibly breaking up with her and
while you're there she'll pop pills, drink scotch
and try to throw herself off the balcony and Taffy
will grab her, slap her and tell her
Nummy isn't worth it.

Then,
Sharon's parents come home and the hysteria is over,
her father's a doctor — a tall, balding somewhat
lecherous-looking doctor, and the house is full of glass
and mirrors, brass trays, carved tiki heads,
exotic   weird   what people collect
when they travel around the world,
bring home and put in glass cabinets
and on coffee tables,
and Sharon's mother has dark hair and a strange
attachment to a little dog, probably a Shih Tzu and
she cannot be bothered until she attends to it.

On the hill against the green sky,
Nummy waits for all the rich kids
to swing by on their way to
build bonfires on the beach, and get high,
and all the kids on the hill are rich.
The sun is an orange slice above the sea
as Nummy sits in the GTO,
his voice slow   slurred,
his white hair falls into his eyes and he offers
you a lude, a peyote button, maybe some windowpane,
you say no thanks and Taffy pulls you away
and you know he likes you but let's face it you
and Taffy just spent hours dealing with his ex-girlfriend's
overdose, he's just too scary and it won't last that long,
he'll be over and it's all mixed up
and crazy and you'll go home to your boyfriend anyway.

You drive back over dark hills through a fading light
to Taffy's big glass condo,

past the swimming pool that's a joke
since you've got the ocean and Taffy's tired
from having to save her friend's life
and you go into her room,
and fall asleep in the over air-conditioned
room and sleep till noon and time to go back
to the beach and another day of sun burning.

When you get home your boyfriend comes
over and the two of you sit in his car having
contests to see who can pull the longest piece
of dried up and peeling skin off your legs.
It doesn't hurt at all. The strips are brown
and crackly, all that great sunbathing being stripped
away leaves your legs with a strange pattern.
You're fascinated by this;
it's an obsession and every morning
you wake up and pull the covers back
to see one layer peeling away
and another underneath emerging soft and new.

Sky

The sky is flat and gray as long haired girls go by
on bikes and the wind pulls at their scarves.
Tulip bulbs rest in the icy soil several streets over.
When I walk by I am eight months pregnant.
I love wandering in the fog where there is no one
but the mailman.

My coat is big. No one can tell that I am pregnant.
I walk and walk in the heavy coat winding through
streets and fog uncertain of time, but certain of my body
as it moves taking long strides. Without the heaviness of the coat
I would not be walking; too light, I would float away.
Even though the baby is there inside me
with her own weight, her own little movements,
that is not enough to keep me on the ground.

In our house it is different. The furniture, dining table,
the lamp, all anchor me in this life that involves the past.
And the past is so full of everything, not just of memory,
but of real things that have found their way into the present.
I don't know which I like best, the present with its past objects
sitting in every corner of the room, or the present with its
nothingness beyond each footstep.

I told my mother about this odd feeling
of being weightless with the baby.
Just me and the baby floating
in a present moment world.
That's when she gave me the coat.
The baby's father is with us. But for some reason

it seems like just the two of us.
The baby and I spend a lot of time alone in our
private world of light and heat, of occasional jabs,
and soft whispers inside me.

The Woman Next Door

The woman next door, who might be considered a friend,
shuts the door after her husband leaves. She dodges questions,
answers and her husband's fists. Then sits in her backyard later
under the grapefruit tree. I have spent an afternoon with her
under the tree. She does not want to talk about the black eye
or the bruise on her arm. I'm not sure what I can do;
this is new for me. It frightens me, something I had heard
about but was never close to. Sometimes we have a drink
in the afternoon, grapefruit juice and vodka.
But the taste of alcohol doesn't really appeal to me now,
probably because of the baby.

Grief and Deception

Summer passes quickly in an apricot of light,
a mild beach wind
tugs my umbrella and for a moment I see them,
children, playing on pavement and the image of
my daughter   (a two-year old, disappeared
at dusk, her tricycle overturned on the sidewalk,
wheels spinning as I ran from house to house searching for her
and though I found her safely in a neighbor's living room,
the image rises up, hot and gutsy, to disturb)

A man asks for money and at first
I say "no" but later, I hand him a croissant, overcompensating for my
          deceit
          (remember the trip to Yosemite and panhandling for kicks
           not for food, and I figure I owe him something,
           see the difference between then and now,
           what you want and what you get,
           see the gap that opens over time.)

As the waitress spills coffee on my shirt
I laugh, thankful at least that I am not still waiting table,
          (although it was not that long ago)
I refuse her offer to pay the cleaning bill and address her as an equal
at which point she pulls out photos of two blonde boys
and their loser father   (her word, not mine)
and I recommend a self-help text   (whose title I've forgotten
                    and the trendiness of which has passed)
She is grateful.
and I might even enable the deception further
by paying her cab fare home or offering
to pay for a community college class

(it was good enough for me
and after all, everyone must get ahead.)

Get away from my other life of ponytail,
whiny husband unsuspecting in a chaos of underwear
and chin stubble,
the never-ending football game

and Saturday shambles
        (learning from the wrong man how to be a husband
        the neighbor gets drunk, hits his wife,
        comes out to rev up the truck and speed away,
        later, she appears bruised and wistful)

One night we lay in the grass
looking at stars, *let's have another baby* he said
but only once, never again   (I was gone by then)
until then, I rode my bicycle around the neighborhood,
waved to the old ladies sitting in lawn chairs.

And now in this strange desert city,
my beach towel dries on the fence in the hot evening air,
particles of bleached sun have attached to me,
like mica, a shiny, delicate light transforming my skin...
each night I begin to write a letter home,
        (no return address, certain it will never be delivered)
to answer my mother's questions,
        Why did you go so far away? Why don't you come home now?
These questions no longer have an answer
but deserve one just the same.

The Baby and Her Shadow

(for Victoria)

She whimpers   frowns
points to the broom,
wants me to sweep
the dark thing away   until
I unfold my hand into first
a bird, then a dog, then a crocodile.
Her startled eyes close   open
at the glittering figures
behind each crevice as my hand,
outstretched into light
changes shape   jumps back,
and I hold her in my arms against
the dark cloth that moves and forms
itself around us
until we are safe on the brick porch,
a hard edge against fear,
a recognizable whole thing.

Becoming Japanese...Interrupted

for my daughter

Four young Japanese women
sit in front of me
taking an English exam,
one takes out a pencil box
and its lime green cover
with pink trim reminds me
of Hello Kitty!
and my daughter who did not complete
her process of becoming Japanese...

The girl closest to me
writes in characters
on the backside of the blue book,
calculating in her first language
what she must say in her second,

this girl was not even born   [when my daughter and I climbed the
          stairs in Japan Town
          to buy Hello Kitty! notepads, pens and pencil box, and
          later, sipped tea and read fortune cookies, believing their
          happy lies]
The girl in the pink jacket
consults her e-dictionary
searching for the correct word,
this girl
was a petal falling on snow
in a country wrapped in silence
          [when Hello Kitty!
          waved to us at the Cherry Blossom Festival,

and my daughter, aged seven, marched by
in her kimono singing to Kyoto flute and drum,
learned to bow, to fold paper,
learned finally to read]

These young women do not smile easily
when I make a joke
or caution them against
being merely correct.
They take refuge in details
        intricacies of line,
                movement of water
                        across stone…
        my daughter's smile comes back to me
as she pours tea and explains the
advantage of Hello Kitty! over others
the brightly wrapped pencils and
intricately designed notepads
and at some point as she talks
[I think her hands will turn
into paper birds
long-necked cranes that float
away in the red-satin wind.]
One young woman
looks up with a smile,
is her smile deep rooted
in the life she left behind,
the weight of it coalescing
as she sketches
a new language onto paper,
then
        gently erases
                the other.

[O-KA-SA-UN]
>the sound falls on me
>in morning sunlight.
>My daughter stares down at me
>in half sleep as I try to pronounce it…
>No! M O T H E R, she repeats
>I try again…
>No!
>Again,
>an awkward word
>turning into a block
>of stone in my mouth
>and I wonder how long
>before the words become
>stones on the path that
>carry her away from me…

Can something be heavy
and light at the same time?

We are heavy and light
packing bags to take flight
from burdens that fall
onto the path
in front of us,
each step
>un-binds,
>>un-does
Each translation
>Seed,
>>Tree,
>>>Fire,
>>>>Ash

Each young woman
        passes through
                grows stronger
                        becomes lighter.

Religious G-Spots

for G

For you   truth
the only weapon, glowing like
a religious G spot above
the saints who remain in an eternal
blissed-out euphoria,   kneel, heel,
mud   stone.

You're off to India, the densest, most intricate
of countries   falling backward
as you climb off the train to unravel
the carefully constructed theory about
purification, salvation, and starving children,
their feet haunt you,
sacrificing bread for a richer paradise
of contemplation and denial,
chaos of the soul, prayers to your sons,
who remain in this country as critics
of a dissolute culture,
and then the radiance, the blue pearl
Om Nama Shivaya and the little hand organ.
Dense   elliptical   slice
the music came through the air,
a scythe cutting wheat.

The prophet Mohammed sneaks by
with just the right amount of spritz
for the soul,   wades into the Ganges
waits for the sick and dying to bathe
in the water of the mystical body,

like the reflection you view in windows,
in rearview mirrors, your face,
you once told me you examined
while driving your car off
the road into a ditch.

Jumping Jehosophat!
leader, teacher, your next spiritual fix,
your next entrance into the dissolving form,
wash away past entanglements, delete the clutter,
leave nothing, your voice recorded earlier to signal
your departure. But this isn't getting at it,
the paring down, the lessening as you become
a sliver of wind, a slit in a dress, an aperture
where light escapes, and in reverse,
a crack in a window, a hole the size
of Montana in the fabric of logic,
a magnificent skin of lies.

You seek the very *whatness* of a thing,
the mother   father tongue as you stroll
in the wedge of darkness looking for
the light, holy hands pierced, Jesus
seeking his own mutilation and death
only to be resurrected over and over,
many sequels of a horror movie.
The narrow path where women fold bed linen
rags, scarves, veils that perform double duty
as house   sanctuary, a temporary
and fragile refuge from samsara.

Iridescent beads of sweat rise on your face
and neck as you move into this configuration,

resounding footsteps, voices, names,
all left behind on the train, and before that
the ruined paradise of your great loves, Da Free,
Pir Vilayat, the desert fathers' asceticism,
even after your own life of opposition,
a New England family, your mother a devotee
of Emerson and the transcendentalists.

You've plunged into several truths at once,
branching streams, follow the brook to its source,
seek the sheik, call off the search,
variations on a theme of Buddhists, Hindus,
Jains. Embrace your love, he exists
for you today in the shape of a Sufi, whirling,
unfurling ecstasy.

I wonder if I will see you again.
Small space. You on your prayer rug,
contradiction of spirit and ego,
recite the Bahagavita,
listen to Alice Coltrane,
read Blavatsky,
smoke a cigarette,
fall backward into Buddha's lap
to witness cold truth
having abandoned the physical
trappings of your life,
the beautiful unfaithful husband,
the little house among mesquites,
an immaculate kitchen with only
raw food and purified water,
blessed by supplication,
exact   penetrating,

your manifestation as healer,
hands cupped, warm, fragrant
over the body to move, knead, twist,
reaching depth, reaching and opening into
ledges of sheer pain that strike and flash
but awaken one to other dreams.

Epistle for Gloria

Something told me you should be at home
practicing the violin
preparing a fish stew.
You poured in pieces
of rare white fish
scrod   swordfish
offered them to your daughter.
She was limpid   full of joy
a book child,
she hid among the aging pages of Rocket Woman,
dreamed of fleeing the city in a boat,
carrying her books and a hand mirror.
Tonight she is thinking about the newborn,
tonight she is flipping through the pages
of a magazine and though there is a current
of electricity pulsing through the house,
she insists on reading by candle light.
She is not afraid of the dark or your
absentminded movements through the house.

She looks like Prince Valiant, you whispered
to me of my daughter. She reminds me of
Dostoevsky as a young and nefarious child.
The lights were dim and someone was talking
about the rusty farm tools hanging on the wall.
A baby cried, musicians tuned their fiddles
and your husband had a face, something like
a sloppy hat. You're lucky he said to me and then
you said it. You had a faraway look in your eyes,
and you and he rode off on bicycles into the
fragrant night, your little girl strapped to your back.

I drove the pickup truck. A farmer carrying her
precious pianos to market. Later, stews and soups,
juice and egg creams.

Years later,
you let twin brothers in the front door.
In the deep kitchen light you couldn't tell them apart,
but one had the marble eye of a tiger and one
peeled roses off beer cans.
You were a woman wearing a veil.
The mouth hidden but the eyes set, determined.
The twins stayed only long enough to love you a little
and paint your kitchen green.

There was ivy and clover and long strands of hair
on the kitchen floor. I cut my daughter's hair and
she hid behind the door in shame, pulling at the
short blonde ends.
I sat with her through the rainy season watching your
television, its miniature screen buzzing and snowy.
Your daughter's pet rat ran on his treadmill.

Your eyes were glazed and furious. The man you
were living with went swimming and possibly drowned
although the body never turned up. The hunter's cap
and boots floated to the surface and you knew
he was a real live killer. He had the instruments,
the customs of inbreeding, a dangerous smile, he
understood the word precious and used it against you.

And now the Kleenex box resting on your knees
grows heavier as you cry. Try as you will to

discard things, they keep turning up.

Pin hole.   Aluminum kite.   Cardboard house.   Shoebox.

We were cultivating a mindful approach to living.
Peeking into drawers filled with lost children,
washing out the bathtubs of the well-to-do,
reading our poems to each other at the kitchen table,
harping and chattering like fantails,
making a joyful noise in the ruins that surrounded us.

Our children's legs have the sleeping weight of iron.
Bolt upright in the middle of the night.
Sandbags.
War and more war.
We watch over them. Passing the bread back and forth
between us like dark-eyed starving soldiers.

From now on we will assume different identities.
You will sit by the fire with a strong cup of brandy
and ponder the days' events.
I will leave the crawl space at dusk and stand
in the desert light.

There will be four brightly lit candles.
I'll light them and you, from your window seat
across the continent, must make sure
they don't go out.

Laura Lost in Prague

If I look into the camera
I may find Laura, her large hazel eyes staring back at me,
looking up from the grey streets of Prague,
no one's heard from her for a decade. I will buy her book,
The Cities of Madame Curie, and pass it into clandestine hands.

In the photo,
boys with thick black bangs,
velvet bow ties, raise aperitif glasses,
toasting a chartreuse sky
and Laura
among the remains,
a chess game, shabby tables of spilled coffee
and electricity sparking in the corners of the room.

The room is bare and grey
a nightclub singer's dressing room,
and Chopin being played on a child's toy piano,
the rough crowd staggers in from the rough streets,
the newest generation of thrill seekers shows up
too late to avoid harm,
it arrives quickly,
a melancholy bride.

In this room Laura said yes,
she undressed by the window,
she spoke out of turn,
she was wrong, she was too old to act like that,
her skin was music that drifted through the cities of Madame Curie,
a window of black telephones,
children warning the authorities that things were out of control,

she came along just at the right time,
she came up short, and saw that the children were already old.
Her city was an engine of loss.
There was a roar in the distance
and she left her room to see what it was.

Vigilance

Somewhere in the older part of the cemetery
my great-grandparents lie in very old clothes
turning to crackly paper because coffins
were not made air tight 100 years ago.
The headstones are huge, casting the shadows
of cherubs curled in marble robes,
gold filigree, birds darting toward heaven
with silk banners in their beaks, but the coffins
were fragile and splintery. Now, coffins are guaranteed
to withstand floods, earthquakes,
small nuclear disasters and deliberate disinterment,
perhaps for an autopsy of some kind,
an old crime unearthed along with the fleeting bones
and clues to a crime that might have occurred
at the very end of a life.

A life in which my uncle died and my aunt
couldn't think of any reason to stay and
so found a way not to.   We all want to blame
the grandson who took her possessions
and made promises he did not keep.
When she died suddenly, he returned her to us
in a wooden box and everyone became hysterical
at the implication that she would actually
be buried in such a contraption.
They all hurried to the telephone,
my mother, her brother, my aunt,
to plead with the heartless and suspect
grandson to return her special knick-knacks
and the ceramic swans with gold leaf wings
and the Christmas elves in their little red pajamas

that are by now worth plenty, and the pictures
of Edwardian couples dancing in bleak ballrooms.
But he refused.
There will be no autopsy,
it is too late. She was promptly moved
to an air-tight upscale model costing at least $6,000.
The only way for the family to rest in peace over the incident.

And so now with my aunt safely tucked
into a blue and silver coffin with birds
engraved alongside to escort her home,
we come to view the face we knew so well,
but is less recognizable now, the forehead almost
too large, the face and mouth hard in death.
She had been beautiful with large hazel eyes,
and full red lips, a severe kind of beautiful.

On the drive home, my mother leans against me,
places her hand on mine as it trembles.
She can't believe her sister is gone,
the one who took care of her when
she was little because their mother
was already too ill to do so. The one she argued
with constantly, the one she called her best friend.
The one who married at fifteen,
divorced and married and had a son,
a beautiful boy everyone called Sonny.
Sonny was the grandson's father, and he died
long before she did, long before his son really knew him.

My mother leans on me now,
her hand shakes against mine, I feel her fear,
her sadness, a second pulse bearing down,
trying to overtake me, to be carried along with my own velocity.

Ten of the Fourteen Miracles

(there is a great discrepancy in the number of miracles attributed to
the Virgin of Guadalupe)

The Virgin of Guadalupe squeezes with thumb and forefinger
each plastic deer, the plastic elves, metal tulips, and blows a kiss
in the direction of three dirt encrusted vans.

Across the street, she jumps the chain link fence, to nap on a battered sofa
wet from afternoon rain. A For Sale sign hides her smiling countenance.

A black pit bull stands at the fence snarling as La Virgen Morena passes
chanting a Nahuatl prayer.

Playground, rubbery fake black top to absorb shock.
A young Mexican woman squats at the bottom of a slide
as the apparition passes dragging a train of sun,
moon, stars behind her.

The Woman of the Apocalypse lies face down in wet grass
where she fell last night out of the boy's pocket, to be trampled, forgotten.
Still she has her world of small creatures to serve.

Outside the laundromat, a black woman, head in a dirty grey turban,
begs, sees the chain, *whats 'is*, she says, turning it over in her palm,
finds the virgin in calm repose at the other end.

Plasma Center, and the virgin contemplating the needles of the agave
and the line of men and women, their cigarette smoke,
their long gray wait becomes a blue-green mantle
stretching for blocks into the path of…

The Yoga practitioners who arrive on bikes or by foot
for the early morning Vinyasa session, feel the veil
that both separates and joins them to the men
and women across the street.

The yoga girl accidentally slips through the veil
the first time and finds a field of brown and white women
exposing the dirt with shovels and rakes.

The white yoga girl honors the color adjustment,
the art of La Virgen Morena,
and women, not more than four or five in a space,
drawing ahead of the dark.

Woman Falling

The house had become a beautiful cage with its wrought iron fence
and big green spacious yard and the fountains that no longer
worked and yet were reminiscent of a time when they did,
and people spilled water on the ground like it was nothing,
and she was from California and so it was easy to understand
the casualness of water, its consolation, its necessity,
and its luxury all at once. She sat gazing out the window
and everything was deliciously calling her and although
it was no longer California and she was a woman slowly falling,
she would remain upright and as long as possible go out into
the white streaked day under water blue sky. Perhaps walk
along a river that was submerged long ago. To walk would
give her the feeling of moving through and over space and time,
and that lovely feeling of movement jostled her into the belief
that she was endless as the landscape splintered into tiny
increments. She ignored it mostly and kept moving,
her feet on the ground; this was the best way to pass time.

And so her day began with new feet, buds and springs.
She wondered about the seasons as she kept pace
with other living things, the trees softly bending
to the ground, the boys on skateboards crashing by,
the runners with sweaty skin passing, and the old man
pushing a stroller with groceries in it. Like a caravan of travelers,
she pretended they were on their way to greet the messiah,
the Buddha, the child savior who told stories about bugs
and sucked on a lollipop through the telling and dripped
the funny red cherry flavored goo onto her dress.
The dress was covered in big pink roses and horses glided
above the mountains, yes children were capable of bringing
such concepts to life. There was a small window

through which the child could see these things but only
for a short time and so she kept moving toward the child,
and the window, and the short span of time.

Chickens on the Avenue

She left the house around two just walking to the Market.
It was a 10 minute walk and she walked slowly.
She walked down the alley. She liked the alleys here
but they weren't actually alleys; they were considered
avenues, Railroad, Bean, Arizona, and Herbert.
They had houses on them facing into and right
onto the roadway which was the size of an alley,
but they weren't alleys and people became very
upset when you called their avenue an alley,
and threatened to call in the Historic Preservation Society.
People set out their trash cans on these avenues
and left them there and there were some neighbors
who went door to door and asked people to take
their trash cans off the avenue. Some did because
they wanted to live on an avenue and not an alley.
But it didn't really last long because few people
who lived on these avenues owned their own home
and few really cared whether it was an alley or
an avenue. Many were students who would have
enjoyed living on an alley for its rundown and picturesque
elements such as crumbling walls and porches,
caved in roofs, broken windows with cardboard
replacement. Some were long-time low-income
residents who liked the old way of living, pretending
they were still in a small town with a real community.
They walked everywhere they went, grew vegetables
in a square foot garden, and fed the pigeons each
morning, causing a violent fluttering of wings when
passersby scared them off.

As she approached 13th Street and Railroad Avenue,

she noticed two chickens in the alley squawking
and clucking around the trash cans and she smiled
because it was fun to see these chickens, these
funny birds clucking around like musical toys
and cartoon characters. She wanted to see more
chickens on the avenue, more funny looking animals
whirling and spinning, having a good time in the sunshine.
The mottled white feathered chicken ducked under
the fence and went into the yard it must have come
from, but the red-feathered chicken hung out
across the road prancing around the trash can,
peered at her, and even greeted her with a squawk.
She would like to own a chicken and not just eat them.
It seemed okay to eat chickens. Everyone said they
had no personality, no intelligence and yet she could
see a playfulness, a glint of mischief in the eye
of the red feathered herky jerky chicken.

Jump

All night men and women cling to the sides of a rattling box car
waiting until it slows to make the crazy turn
in the warehouse district. When it does, they jump
off the train into deep weeds and run through the neighborhood.
As I dream, it seems they run across my bed,
movements so light
when they run through
windy grass to another hand reaching out,
they are silent. Then I wake to the squealing iron wheels of the train.

I watch them go by,
two men, a man and woman,
a woman and three young girls.
Quick movements, heads down, wrinkled clothes,
heavy packs, these things give them away.
A mother, wrapped snugly in a long red skirt,
hair pulled back, doesn't look up. But one of her daughters does.
She looks directly into my eyes to make sure that I see her.

Pablo

for Pablo Neruda

When Pablo died she was riding the bus through fog
across the Bay Bridge and reading *The Disinherited* by Jack Conroy.
She was unaware of Pablo's death at the time but there was
something she felt, a shift; she looked up and out across
the Bay but could only see the steel girders, a gray sky,
and cars rushing into the city. This was her beginning
in many ways. She climbed out at the bus station and
walked two blocks to her new job, a place without poetry,
a place of pennies and nickels dropped in the coffee kitty,
a place of refugees and poor women. A place Pablo would
have told a story about, a political manifesto, or a sad love
poem wringing the stars from the sky. Although she knew
Pablo, he did not know her, not in fog, or in the fields that
stretched toward a trampled sky. Some fear was good she
would learn, on her bus ride back and forth to the city each
day, that what she saw was what he might have seen or written.
She walked through the bus depot past others who made
it their home, on hard plastic benches and cold concrete,
wrapped in layers of sweaters and dirty jackets, abandoned,
wounded, having fallen there. But she would keep walking.
The magnificent ocean sparkled just over hills at the end of land.
It was good to witness what could happen, as Pablo had,
even in the most beautiful of places.

Falling

(thanks to Laurie Anderson)

The day had gone perfectly
when she started to think about the eclipse,
or the laundry or the weeds, she simply
shut it out of her mind and kept going up
the hill in the sunlight and she did a U turn
and found the parking lot under Mesquite.
There were others there already, jogging, biking,
walking along the River that actually did flow and glisten,
the ends of dead trees sticking up out of the mud
and she headed away from the overpass.
The noise, the machines were never far away.
She thought about the impression she was making
in the ground, the other feet that had walked
this ground, the Mormon settlers, the Apache,
the cavalry. But she couldn't quite capture
the feeling on the asphalt trail. And the river
was a shallow stream and in a few weeks
would disappear under the sand. But not before
a full moon bobbled in the water, and perhaps
someone would be there to see it. Some ghost
animal to move through the muddy rushes
to witness the strange people who rode bicycles
up and down and walked back and forth all day
with nowhere to go. She liked the neverendingness
of the trail, a story that unfolded but had to be built
and rebuilt and this time the path was so well kept
and tended all the way to the horizon.
She tried to blot out the apartment buildings,
housing developments, business parks,

and to think only of what had been here before.
Two hundred years ago, the laundress hung
the clothing in the trees and went back to her tub.
Birds chirped and twittered reminding her of Apaches
and the snow prints, the dark smudges under
the eyes and crazy falling stars they lived their lives by.
The neverendingness of her legs moving,
pulling, digging into the gravel, crunch crunch
across the sand and rocks. And each time she
took a step she realized she was also falling
forward into the unknown.

Water Is the World's Consolation

the back stroke at night   looking up into the sky
           a dark net of shattered glass
water laps   a warm breeze drifts across your nose,

smelling,
     breathing in
          the stars, the sky, the underwater lights,
and the breeze
          that has passed through the limbs

of mesquite trees
     creosote bushes
an intense gold-green scent that sweeps everything
clean,

water is memory of drinking down the world,
full immersion into the dark stream,
for a moment your grandmother's dress billows
     in water,
your mother wipes away tears and the sticky
residue of leaves,
confrontation of water and flesh
discrete   moments of solitude,

your chest aches and thumps,
the damp hair under your cap is electric and tingly
     as you drift until you reach the other side

your hand touches the concrete wall
a deep dense odor of wet pavement
     playing in the streets after a summer rain,

the hot asphalt steams under your tennis shoes
as you cross the street to find your friend.

Narcissus in the Desert

She arrives early
with the first threads of light,
entering the water in a way that
creates triangles and rectangles on her body.
She swims slowly,
thinking through each moment
of this confrontation of water and flesh.
A finger of light comes through the water,
she reaches up with one arm,
stretches up then arcs for a moment
before slipping back down
and under,
pulling her body through
the color almost scarlet where her hands
stretch across and into the water.

Water that has been trapped in her ear drips out onto the towel where she lays.
There is a pop and a whoosh — then the sounds of the lifeguard's whistle and the
squeal of laughter at the shallow end.

***

He walks by flexing his back,
has let his hair grow longer,
just enough
so the wind can ruffle the front.
He finds a lounge chair at the far end of the deck
        and lies down. He has a book with him,
is rarely without one
but she knows he isn't really reading.
Soon he gets up, dangling his goggles.

He does a thorough scan of the deck
to make sure everyone can see him
but he does this in such a way
that he will not have to look
directly at anyone, nor will he be accused
of caring at all that others are watching him.
He wraps his arms around his chest,
letting his hands slap against his upper back,
takes several large steps backward,
then runs toward the lane
and jack knifes [very high] into the water.
His goggles float in the shallow overflow...
as he does his first lap without them,
a long beautiful freestyle in very slow strokes.

***

The boy's chest shimmers
from the previous day's sunbathing
and this makes his bright blue eyes
more startling against his burnished cheeks...
He smiles at her as he walks by,
a smile that is practiced,
trained.
He is small
with a lean bird like body.
As he steps into the water, beads
reflecting sunlight cling
to his dark curls and skin.
His freestyle is smooth   clean.
His backstroke is tentative   choppy.
She remembers being told to keep
her arms as straight as possible,

that the little finger should enter the water first,
yet his arms bend at the elbow,
his hands enter the water at an odd angle
creating a shadow against the sunlight.
The shadow follows him
up and down the lane as he disappears in water.

***

A new lifeguard is working the afternoon shift,
his skin so white, she wonders
if he has just moved to the desert from
some cold sunless country.
He has chin length red hair,
a freckled complexion, full red lips.
He is small   with a tough
working-class persona,
a lunch pail lifeguard who stares
at the swimmers openly, contemptuously.
He climbs into his chair   no hat   no sunglasses, defying
the caustic rays of the sun. He sits in a slightly slumped down
position that suggests discomfort, even embarrassment,
then slowly he lets his slender white legs splay out and he
seems to surrender to the water below,
the scent of chlorine rises,
wrapping him in its funky perfume.

***

He is very tall with
bronze apple deltoids
resting above his biceps,
a flat wall of a chest

and the outline of his ribs
etched perfectly underneath.
She has watched him turn varying shades
from coffee and cream, to burnished with a hint of copper,
to bronze. The gold flecks rise off his skin
as he climbs out of the water
and begins stroking the glistening indentation
between his chiseled pecs,
aware that he is being watched.

***

His twin   with a softer face
a mole on his left cheek   is bored.
He slams the volleyball against a wall
as hard as he can, over and over
making the sound reverberate through the pillars
and bounce across the water.
In a movement suggesting weariness,
he turns to eye two girls who are sunbathing nearby.
When they rise to leave, he turns again,
this time to his twin
and they nod their approval at one another.

***

At precisely 3:00 in the afternoon and 107 degrees...
he drapes his towel across
one of the lounge chairs.
His bathing suit is a perfect square
of red, black, and white stripes
covering his neat little frame.
The suit looks like the blanket

in Rousseau's *Sleeping Gypsy*.
She hides behind a pillar out of the sun,
but can still feel the heat radiating
off the deck. It makes her face hot.
She closes her eyes,
takes six deep breaths, then opens them,
unable to concentrate.
She peeks around the pillar and sees him
lying face up in full sun
unaware of the danger he is in.
He is slim and perfect on the white lounge.
His skin a dark coffee bean color
and even beyond this,
gradations of tone and depth
giving way to slate gray under his ribs,
and across his neck where shadows fall.

***

He kicks off his sandals,
begins organizing his pool supplies,
suntan lotion, shades, CD player, bathing cap,
goggles, and towel. She has seen him many times at the pool,
each time in a different bathing suit,
each one more daring than the last.
He has advanced from a standard Speedo
to a woman's one- piece fitted in navy blue,
to a suit with just the hint of a skirt.
She has seen his body become supple
although she has not seen him
actually do any swimming.
He walks to the pool edge,
casts a glance at the new lifeguard

whose hair is aflame now
in mid-afternoon sun.
He stands under the lifeguard tower,
his towel wrapped around the lower half of his body.
She watches. He waits.
Suddenly he pulls the towel off
and she sees the hot-pink thong
as he quickly plunges into water.
In an almost imperceptible movement,
the lifeguard turns to look
and she sees his jaw muscles tighten.

***

She applies an extra coating of sun block,
settles herself comfortably away
from the noise of other swimmers.
He comes through the locker room door
carrying two green duffle bags.
She watches out of the corner of her eye,
to see which direction he will take
and sees he is coming straight towards her,
the deep end   a scuba diver,
tall with perfectly formed arms and legs,
long ropy muscles,
his wide chest   open and receptive,
his stride   relaxed but not loose,
his chin at a perfect 90 degree angle,
his gaze straight ahead,
although she knows he sees her.
He drops one bag,
begins carefully unpacking the other,
fins, weight belt, a tank, mask, and tube.

His back is to her and as he bends over in front of her
she notices that his black swim trunks
are loose near the crotch
and the edge of his white jock strap
can just be seen.
She looks away, surprised by this laxity.
Everything else about him speaks precision,
from his round buzz cut
with tiny glints of silver at the temples,
to his feet with their perfect arches.
Soon two other men join him...
older, shorter, heavier   his coaches.
He stands, as though at attention,
listening to their directives   *You were with the Rescue Warriors, right?*
From the side his pecs look like small breasts,
and this makes him seem vulnerable.

She closes her eyes...   hears only the water rushing up and into the spill over;
wind picks up the voices and carries them away.

***

Two girls wrapped in purple shawls
tiptoe to the shallow end   then slip in
shedding their thin garments. Their hair is long
pulled back,   but not neatly   thick unruly strands
find their way out of the bands that hold them
and float on top of the water as the girls dog-paddle in circles.
They giggle and splash, never going all the way under.
Soon they are joined by a very tall
dark-skinned young man who saunters toward them
in strides that are at once graceful and sloppy.
As he dives in   they surround him   catching him

in their circle of blue water   black hair. One of the girls picks him up
trying to hold him like a child in her arms,
but his weight causes her to fall backwards
and as she does,   he jerks upright   laughing
wiping water out of his eyes.
Then both girls make a bridge for his body
with their arms and he lays down across them
as they walk with him through the water.
He pretends to fight them   to struggle free
but it is all artifice as they laugh
turn in circles   tighten their grip.
Yellow circles of sunlight bounce
as blue water begins to churn with their movements
their bodies   and his long brown legs gently kicking
until he surrenders in their arms.

Lap swimmers swim back and forth with precision and determination
          turning their heads from side to side, mouths gasping for air; they
     do not see the small whirlpool of delight at the shallow end.

Little Lost Things

The girl's mother's poem
>that went into a book with a thousand other poems, a book
>the mother couldn't afford to purchase.

The red earring
>that fell behind the dresser, but when the dresser was moved,
>it wasn't there because it had fallen into a hole in the wood
>behind the dresser and there really wasn't a way to get it
>because jewelry bounces when it hits the floor.

The keys
>a whole set of keys, were dropped somewhere on Spring Mountain,
>lost keys and the friendship that went with it, and

the incredible Bakelite bracelet and earrings
>see-through blue with purple flowers inside that must be worth
>at least $500.00 by now.

The books Charles made
>cartoon drawings of me and my daughter, and him
>with his red hair and black stove-pipe hat; the books
>are gone and so is Charles, off to LA, then off of the earth.

The necklace with copper softball
>I got for being the pitcher on the girls' championship team
>one summer.

My father's tie
>with green and orange cowboy hats on it.

The old chest
>a stack of starched aprons inside, and possibly the tie, but we never
checked.

A short story
>about my grandmother described as a gambler and a drinker
and which Charles said was not a story, at least not yet.

A Terri Lee doll
>dismembered, lying in pieces in a cardboard box.

Sandra Cantu
>accidentally killed, stuffed into a suitcase and left by a canal bank.

The cigarette butt
>he flicked out the window of the hospital that traveled
through the cold air hissing, landing
like a tiny missile in the rose bushes.

A tiny silk handkerchief
>that blew off the hat, that fell off the wall.

The bracelet
>with sea charms, anemone, starfish, urchin, marble shell,
sand dollar, a bracelet that had been stolen
from a jewelry counter in 1967.

Lost, falling, windswept pieces
>of light and metal slipping through the shipwrecked arms
of a stranger now.

A silver bracelet
      with black stones belonging to my mother who was dying,
      stolen from a yard sale by someone
      with no attachment to the bracelet or my mother.

Sandra Florence

received her Masters in English/Creative Writing from San Francisco State University, and has been writing and teaching in Tucson, Arizona for the last thirty-three years. She taught at the University of Arizona for 18 ½ years and in a number of community education settings working with refugees, the homeless, adolescent parents, women in recovery and juveniles at risk. She is the recipient of a National Endowment for the Humanities grant under the initiative The National Conversation on American Pluralism and Identity, and through the grant ran a community writing project for 2½ years. She has published scholarly articles on writing and healing and writing as a tool for public dialogue. She currently teaches writing and literature at Pima Community College. This is her first book-length collection of poetry.

www.ingramcontent.com/pod-product-compliance
Lightning Source LLC
Chambersburg PA
CBHW080514110426
42742CB00017B/3106